Prompts & Circumstances
500 Talking Points on Social Climate Issues

GENT HOGAN

PROMPTS & CIRCUMSTANCES 500 TALKING POINTS ON SOCIAL CLIMATE ISSUES

SOCIAL ISSUES

Category 1: Personal Empowerment and Growth Mindset & Resilience Talking Points (1–25) Example: "Resilience is not just about bouncing back but adapting forward." "Growth starts where comfort ends." Overcoming Adversity Talking Points (26–50) Example: "Adversity is a call to action for creativity and perseverance." The Role of Education in Personal Growth Talking Points (51–75) Example: "Education is a tool for liberation, not just information."

Category 2: Spiritual Awakening Living Between Dimensions Talking Points (76–100) Example: "Synchronicities are whispers from the universe; pay attention." Spirituality vs. Religion Talking Points (101–125) Example: "Spirituality connects; religion often divides—what bridges the gap?" Integrating Spiritual Awakening into Daily Life Talking Points (126–150) Example: "The awakened soul finds purpose in every task, no matter how small."

Category 3: Relationships Unpacking Modern Relationship Dynamics Talking Points (151–175) Example: "Boundaries in relationships are a sign of respect, not rejection." Gender Roles and Expectations Talking Points (176–200) Example: "Feminine and masculine energies are complements, not competitions." Dating in the Digital Age Talking Points (201–225) Example: "Swipe culture has commodified love; how do we bring back depth?"

Category 4: Identity and Society Black Identity and Representation Talking Points (226–250) Example: "Representation in media is not diversity; it's the start of inclusion." Cultural Pressures and Respectability Politics Talking Points (251–275) Example: "Respectability politics are a survival tool, but do they serve growth?" The Intersection of Colorism and Privilege Talking Points (276–300) Example: "Colorism isn't just about skin tone; it's about power dynamics."

Category 5: Social and Economic Structures The Wealth Gap and Generational Cycles Talking Points (301–325) Example: "Generational wealth starts with generational education." Education and Its Societal Impacts Talking Points (326–350) Example: "Standardized testing is a measure of privilege, not potential." Gentrification and Its Double Edges Talking Points (351–375) Example: "Gentrification can build communities or displace them—what's the balance?"

Category 6: Feminism and Masculinity Modern Feminism vs. Traditional Roles Talking Points (376–400) Example: "Feminism isn't about rejecting men but rejecting oppression." Toxic Masculinity and Its Healing Talking Points (401–425) Example: "Toxic masculinity isn't about men being bad; it's about harmful conditioning."

Category 7: Youth and Elders The Generational Divide Talking Points (426–450) Example: "Wisdom isn't outdated; it's just waiting for the right ears." Social Media's Influence on the Younger Generation Talking Points (451–475) Example: "The algorithm isn't neutral; it reflects and shapes culture." The Role of Elders in Modern Society Talking Points (476–500) Example: "Elders are the keepers of tradition; how do we invite them back to the table?"

INTRODUCTION

Purpose of the Book
This book is designed as a comprehensive guide to navigating and contributing to discussions on pressing social climate issues. This is a guidebook for thought leaders, panelists, hosts, educators, and individuals who wish to deepen their understanding of societal challenges and inspire meaningful conversations. This book provides talking points and reflective prompts that encourage critical thinking and foster solutions that lead to growth, empathy, and change.

This guide is a practical tool for approaching complex topics, whether hosting a panel discussion, curating content for social media, or engaging in one-on-one conversations.

How to Use This Guide

1. **Panel Discussions:**

    - Each section is designed to facilitate dynamic, thought-provoking dialogue. Use the talking points to introduce topics, prompt discussions, and guide debates.
    - Encourage panelists to bring unique perspectives, incorporating their experiences and expertise.
    - Pair talking points with the follow-up questions provided to spark deeper engagement.

2. **Social Media Conversations:**

    - Social media thrives on concise, impactful messaging. Use the talking points as standalone posts, discussion starters, or video scripts.

    ◦ Include reflective questions to invite audience participation and create meaningful interactions.

3. **Personal Growth and Learning:**

    ◦ Reflect on the talking points as part of your journey toward understanding social issues.

    ◦ Use the follow-up questions and suggested prompts to journal, meditate, or spark conversations within your community.

4. **Educators and Advocates:**

    ◦ Adapt the talking points for classroom discussions, workshops, or training sessions.

    ◦ Use them to create lesson plans or activities to encourage critical thinking and empathy.

The Importance of Critical Thinking in Social Climate Conversations

This era is fast information and polarized opinions and critical thinking is essential. It empowers us to:

- **Discern Fact from Opinion:** Evaluate the validity of arguments and avoid falling prey to misinformation.
- **Foster Empathy:** Understand different perspectives and engage with others respectfully, even when disagreements arise.
- **Find Solutions:** Move beyond identifying problems to collaborate and develop actionable steps for change.
- **Break Echo Chambers:** Challenge our biases and open ourselves to diverse viewpoints.

CATERGORY ONE: Personal Empowerment and Growth

MINDSET & RESILIENCE

Talking Points (1–25):

1. "Resilience is not just about bouncing back but adapting forward."
2. "Growth starts where comfort ends."
3. "Your mindset shapes your reality; a growth mindset creates endless possibilities."
4. "Failures are stepping stones, not tombstones."
5. "Self-doubt is the biggest thief of potential—conquer it with action."
6. "Resilience is a skill, not an innate trait. It can be learned and strengthened."
7. "Challenges are opportunities to practice strength and adaptability."
8. "A resilient mindset sees setbacks as setups for comebacks."
9. "Your thoughts are seeds—plant positivity and watch resilience grow."
10. "Reframing problems as puzzles to solve builds mental endurance."
11. "The ability to pause and reflect is a hallmark of a resilient mind."

12. "You are not your circumstances; you are how you respond to them."
13. "Resilience thrives in community—lean on others when needed."
14. "Belief in your ability to change is the foundation of resilience."
15. "Letting go of what you can't control is key to maintaining inner strength."
16. "Every storm leaves behind lessons for growth; learn to harvest them."
17. "A resilient person doesn't avoid fear—they confront and transcend it."
18. "Adaptability is the bridge between resilience and success."
19. "Resilience requires rest—burnout is the enemy of long-term strength."
20. "Mindset shifts happen one thought at a time; be patient with the process."
21. "Optimism fuels resilience, but realism guides it."
22. "A positive mindset doesn't ignore problems—it tackles them creatively."
23. "Your greatest growth often comes after your greatest challenges."
24. "The stories we tell ourselves about adversity shape our ability to overcome it."
25. "Resilience is the art of thriving despite uncertainty."

OVERCOMING ADVERSITY

Talking Points (26–50):

1. "Adversity is a call to action for creativity and perseverance."
2. "Struggles are proof of progress; stagnation breeds complacency."

3. "The strongest people you know have faced the greatest battles."
4. "Adversity is the furnace where character is forged."
5. "The ability to pivot is essential when plans are derailed."
6. "Every setback holds a seed of opportunity for growth."
7. "The pain of adversity is temporary; the lessons are permanent."
8. "Facing adversity with courage inspires others to do the same."
9. "Adversity doesn't break you—it reveals who you truly are."
10. "Your ability to adapt determines whether adversity defeats or strengthens you."
11. "Turning pain into purpose is a powerful way to overcome adversity."
12. "Every person you admire has faced and conquered significant challenges."
13. "Adversity tests your limits; overcoming it redefines them."
14. "It's not the load that breaks you but how you carry it."
15. "Adversity is a teacher; the question is, are you willing to learn?"
16. "Success is often found on the other side of perseverance."
17. "Adversity reveals hidden strengths you didn't know you had."
18. "Growth through adversity requires both grit and grace."
19. "Vulnerability during hard times is a strength, not a weakness."

20. "Building emotional intelligence helps you navigate adversity with resilience."
21. "Adversity forces you to get creative with solutions."
22. "Seeing challenges as temporary boosts resilience and hope."
23. "A support network can turn adversity into an opportunity for connection."
24. "Adversity prepares you for opportunities you didn't know you needed."
25. "Success is sweeter when you've endured the struggle to achieve it."

THE ROLE OF EDUCATION IN PERSONAL GROWTH

Talking Points (51–75):

1. "Education is a tool for liberation, not just information."
2. "Lifelong learning is the secret to lasting growth."
3. "Formal education opens doors; self-education builds the house."
4. "The more you know, the more you grow."
5. "Education is an investment in yourself that pays dividends for life."
6. "The role of education is to light the fire of curiosity, not extinguish it with conformity."
7. "True education teaches you how to think, not what to think."
8. "Education is the great equalizer; it levels the playing field for all."
9. "Self-education is your responsibility; no one will do it for you."
10. "A thirst for knowledge keeps you young, no matter your age."

11. "Critical thinking is the most valuable skill education can teach."
12. "Education should empower, not indoctrinate."
13. "The purpose of education is to prepare you for a life of contribution."
14. "Knowledge is power, but applied knowledge is freedom."
15. "Your education doesn't end when school does; that's just the beginning."
16. "The best lessons in life often come from experiences, not textbooks."
17. "Education creates opportunities, but effort turns them into achievements."
18. "Don't just learn for yourself—share knowledge to empower others."
19. "A growth mindset transforms failures into valuable lessons."
20. "The best students are those who never stop questioning."
21. "Education is the foundation of personal and societal transformation."
22. "Teaching others what you know solidifies your learning."
23. "Curiosity fuels education; nurture it like a garden."
24. "Reading is a powerful way to expand your perspective and understanding."
25. "The most valuable degrees are the ones that teach resilience and critical thinking."

Subtopic: Overcoming Adversity

Host Script:

"Adversity is inevitable, but how we respond defines us. Let's explore some actionable strategies for overcoming adversity. How can individuals transform challenges into opportunities for growth?"

Talking Points for Panelists:

1. **Adversity as a Teacher:**

    - "Adversity often presents opportunities to develop patience, problem-solving, and self-worth. It forces us to dig deep and uncover strengths we didn't know we had."

2. **The Importance of Community Support:**

    - "Community support is critical in overcoming adversity. We can't always go it alone, and leaning on a network of trusted individuals can make all the difference."

3. **Faith and Spirituality in Adversity:**

    - "The role of faith or spirituality in navigating adversity is often underestimated. A strong spiritual foundation can provide a sense of purpose and resilience during tough times."

4.   **Turning Pain into Purpose:**

   - "Adversity can be the catalyst for finding one's life purpose. Many people channel their struggles into meaningful work that inspires others."

5.   **Adaptability and Flexibility:**

   - "The ability to adapt to changing circumstances is a cornerstone of overcoming adversity. Flexibility in thinking and action can open doors to unexpected solutions."

6.   **Resilience as a Skill:**

   - "Resilience isn't something you're born with—it's a skill you build over time through experiences and intentional practices."

7.   **The Role of Emotional Intelligence:**

   - "Adversity often triggers intense emotions. Developing emotional intelligence helps us regulate our feelings and approach challenges with clarity."

8.   **The Power of Perspective:**

   - "Reframing challenges as opportunities for growth shifts the mindset from victimhood to empowerment."

9.   **Taking Action Over Waiting:**

   - "Action, even small steps, is often the antidote to despair. Moving forward, no matter how slowly, builds momentum."

10.   **The Value of Rest in Adversity:**

> · "Rest and self-care are critical during times of adversity. Burnout only compounds challenges, so taking time to recharge is an act of strength."

Follow-Up Questions:

1. "What is one practice or habit you've found most effective in overcoming adversity?"
2. "How do systemic inequalities exacerbate individual adversity, and what can be done to address them?"
3. "Can you share a personal story of turning pain into purpose?"
4. "How can we build resilience proactively, rather than waiting until adversity strikes?"
5. "What role do mentors or role models play in helping individuals navigate difficult times?"

10 QUICK PROMPT QUESTIONS

Use these as icebreakers, conversation starters, or reflective prompts to spark engaging dialogue:

1. "What's the biggest lesson you've learned from facing adversity?"
2. "How do you define resilience in your own words?"
3. "Can adversity be a blessing in disguise? Why or why not?"
4. "What role does mindset play in overcoming challenges?"
5. "How can we support someone going through a tough time?"
6. "Do you believe hardships build character? Why?"
7. "What's one piece of advice you'd give to someone struggling to move forward?"
8. "How do systemic barriers influence personal resilience?"
9. "What's a moment in your life where you turned a challenge into an opportunity?"
10. "How do faith, spirituality, or belief systems help during difficult times?"

CATERGORY TWO: Spiritual Awakening

Living Between Dimensions

Talking Points (76–100):

1. "Synchronicities are whispers from the universe; pay attention."
2. "Living between dimensions requires a balance between the physical and the spiritual."
3. "You are both a spiritual being having a human experience and a human being discovering your spiritual nature."
4. "The veil between dimensions is thinner than most people realize—intuition is your guide."
5. "Dreams often serve as portals to other dimensions of understanding."
6. "Being spiritually awakened in a physical world can feel isolating; seek community for connection."
7. "Signs from the universe are confirmation that you're aligned with your higher purpose."
8. "Awareness of multiple dimensions brings heightened clarity but also responsibility."
9. "Grounding practices like meditation or time in nature are essential for navigating multidimensionality."
10. "Living between dimensions means learning to trust the unseen."
11. "You're always creating your reality, whether you know it or not."

12. "The heart is the bridge between the physical and spiritual dimensions."
13. "Raising your vibration attracts opportunities aligned with your highest self."
14. "Empathy often increases during spiritual awakening—use it wisely."
15. "Channeling energy from higher dimensions into physical actions creates lasting impact."
16. "Your higher self always knows the way—quiet your mind to hear it."
17. "Balance in the spiritual and physical realms requires honoring both aspects equally."
18. "Living between dimensions is less about escaping reality and enhancing it."
19. "When you align with your higher frequency, relationships and opportunities naturally shift."
20. "Multidimensional living teaches us that time is non-linear—patience is key."
21. "Intuition is the language of the higher dimensions; learn to listen."
22. "You may lose connections as you awaken, but you'll gain deeper, aligned relationships."
23. "Living in two worlds requires courage, authenticity, and trust in divine timing."
24. "Not everyone will understand your journey, but that's okay—it's uniquely yours."
25. "The more aligned you are with your true self, the more seamless your connection between dimensions becomes."

SPIRITUALITY VS. RELIGION

Talking Points (101–125):

1. "Spirituality connects; religion often divides—what bridges the gap?"
2. "Religion often focuses on structure; spirituality encourages exploration."
3. "Spirituality is deeply personal, while religion is often communal."
4. "Dogma can limit growth, but spiritual exploration expands understanding."
5. "Religion seeks salvation; spirituality seeks alignment with the divine within."
6. "Spirituality encourages questions, while religion often relies on answers."
7. "Faith and spirituality can coexist, it requires openness and balance."
8. "Many religious teachings have spiritual truths at their core; discernment is key."
9. "Spirituality honors the diversity of experience, while religion often emphasizes conformity."
10. "Your spiritual journey is not defined by attendance at a place of worship but by your alignment with higher truths."
11. "The essence of spirituality is love; religion sometimes gets lost in rules."
12. "Religion provides a map; spirituality is the journey."
13. "Spirituality allows for direct connection to the divine without intermediaries."
14. "Spirituality embraces the mystical, the unknown, and the universal."
15. "Religion often preserves traditions, while spirituality evolves with the individual."

16. "Both religion and spirituality seek meaning, but their paths differ."
17. "Spirituality fosters unity; religion, at times, has sown division."
18. "Ancient wisdom suggests that spirituality predates organized religion."
19. "Religion can be a gateway to spirituality, but it doesn't have to be the destination."
20. "Spirituality invites you to see yourself as a co-creator with the divine."
21. "Many find freedom in spirituality after feeling constrained by religion."
22. "Spirituality often integrates practices from multiple traditions, enriching the journey."
23. "Religion asks you to believe; spirituality asks you to experience."
24. "When religion and spirituality align, they create powerful transformations."
25. "Ultimately, both paths seek the same goal: connection with the divine."

INTEGRATING SPIRITUAL AWAKENING INTO DAILY LIFE

Talking Points (126–150):

1. "The awakened soul finds purpose in every task, no matter how small."
2. "Spiritual awakening isn't about escaping the world but engaging with it meaningfully."
3. "Daily mindfulness is the foundation of living an awakened life."
4. "Your actions reflect your spiritual growth; live your truth consistently."

5. "Practicing gratitude grounds spiritual awareness in everyday life."
6. "Make time for silence and stillness—your soul needs space to breathe."
7. "Spiritual awakening doesn't end; it deepens with every experience."
8. "Bring your spiritual values into your work, relationships, and decisions."
9. "Service to others is a natural expression of spiritual awakening."
10. "Every challenge is an opportunity to practice spiritual principles."
11. "Balance is key—honor your spiritual needs while meeting physical responsibilities."
12. "Grounding yourself daily helps integrate spiritual insights into action."
13. "Awakening often comes with heightened empathy; use it to uplift others."
14. "Journaling is a powerful tool for processing spiritual insights."
15. "Your spiritual practice doesn't need to be perfect; it needs to be authentic."
16. "Aligning with your higher self means saying no to things that no longer serve you."
17. "Spiritual awakening is not about being 'above' others but walking alongside them with compassion."
18. "Even mundane activities can be spiritual when done with presence and intention."
19. "The true test of awakening is how you handle life's challenges."
20. "Let your spiritual journey inspire others, but don't impose it on them."
21. "Every moment is sacred when viewed through spiritual awareness."

22. "Daily affirmations can help align your thoughts with your higher purpose."
23. "Meditation and breathwork are essential tools for integrating spirituality."
24. "Find spiritual practices that resonate with you, and commit to them consistently."
25. "Living an awakened life is about being in tune with both the divine and the human aspects of yourself."

Subtopic: Spirituality vs. Religion

Host Script:

"Spirituality and religion are often seen as opposites, yet they both seek to connect us to something greater. What are the similarities and differences, and how can they coexist to create a more holistic understanding of the divine?"

Talking Points for Panelists:

1. "Religion provides structure; spirituality offers freedom. Together, they can create a holistic path that combines guidance and personal exploration."
2. "Many people reject religion due to its historical misuse of power but find solace in personal spiritual practices that resonate with their truth."
3. "Spirituality allows for individual exploration and interpretation, while religion often emphasizes communal practices and shared beliefs."
4. "Both religion and spirituality aim to answer life's big questions—purpose, morality, and the nature of the divine."
5. "Spirituality embraces the mystical and universal, while religion often focuses on tradition and doctrine."

Follow-Up Questions:

1. "Do you believe spirituality can thrive without the communal aspects often found in religion?"
2. "How can people reconcile the two in their personal lives to find greater meaning and connection?"
3. "What role do rituals play in bridging the gap between religion and spirituality?"
4. "How can those disillusioned by religion rediscover faith through spirituality?"
5. "Do you think modern spirituality risks losing depth by focusing too much on individualism?"

10 QUICK PROMPT QUESTIONS

1. "What does living between dimensions mean to you, and how do you experience it?"
2. "Can synchronicities guide us, or are they just coincidences? What's your take?"
3. "How do you personally balance spiritual practices with the demands of the physical world?"
4. "Is there a moment in your life when spirituality gave you clarity during a challenging time?"
5. "Do you think spirituality and religion are two sides of the same coin? Why or why not?"
6. "What are practical ways to incorporate spiritual principles into everyday tasks?"
7. "How can someone reconnect with spirituality if they've grown disillusioned with religion?"
8. "What role does community play in your spiritual journey? Is it essential or optional?"
9. "How do you approach conversations about spirituality with those who are deeply religious?"
10. "What's one spiritual practice or belief that has transformed how you see the world?"

CATERGORY THREE: Relationships

UNPACKING MODERN RELATIONSHIP DYNAMICS

Talking Points (151–175):

1. "Boundaries in relationships are a sign of respect, not rejection."
2. "Effective communication is the cornerstone of any healthy relationship."
3. "Empathy allows us to see relationships as partnerships, not power struggles."
4. "Self-awareness is key to building authentic connections with others."
5. "Healthy relationships prioritize mutual growth over individual control."
6. "Love languages highlight that affection is not one-size-fits-all."
7. "Toxic relationships often stem from unhealed wounds—both personal and shared."
8. "Relationships thrive when both individuals are committed to self-improvement."
9. "Conflict in relationships isn't inherently bad; it's how we handle it that matters."
10. "Forgiveness is as much about freeing yourself as it is about repairing the relationship."
11. "Attachment styles deeply influence how we approach intimacy and connection."

12. "Mutual vulnerability fosters deeper trust and understanding."
13. "Healthy relationships require effort but should never feel like constant struggle."
14. "Your relationship with yourself sets the tone for every other connection you have."
15. "Partnerships should enhance your life, not be your entire identity."
16. "Unspoken expectations are often the root of relationship dissatisfaction."
17. "Growing apart is natural if both people aren't growing together."
18. "Trust is built over time but can be shattered in an instant—guard it carefully."
19. "Relationship patterns often reflect childhood dynamics; understanding them is key."
20. "Kindness in relationships is underrated but incredibly powerful."
21. "Boundaries protect emotional safety and enhance intimacy when respected."
22. "Accountability in relationships fosters trust and long-term connection."
23. "Healthy relationships don't require perfection, just consistent effort and care."
24. "Being honest about your needs and desires is an act of love."
25. "Authenticity in relationships allows for deeper, more meaningful connections."

GENDER ROLES AND EXPECTATIONS

Talking Points (176–200):

1. "Feminine and masculine energies are complements, not competitions."

2. "Traditional gender roles are evolving, but expectations can still create pressure."
3. "Empowering both genders leads to healthier, more balanced partnerships."
4. "Men and women are not opposites; they are interdependent in unique ways."
5. "Breaking free from rigid gender roles allows individuals to explore their true selves."
6. "Gender equality in relationships starts with mutual respect and shared responsibility."
7. "Cultural norms often dictate gender roles, but they can be challenged and redefined."
8. "The division of labor in relationships should reflect individual strengths, not stereotypes."
9. "Toxic masculinity and performative femininity hinder authentic connection."
10. "Vulnerability is often stigmatized for men but is essential for emotional intimacy."
11. "Balancing career ambitions with family expectations is a challenge for all genders."
12. "Unlearning societal expectations is a necessary step toward personal growth."
13. "The rise of egalitarian relationships is redefining partnership dynamics."
14. "Traditional masculinity often suppresses emotions, leading to disconnection."
15. "Modern feminism calls for the liberation of all genders, not just women."
16. "Healthy masculinity values strength and sensitivity equally."
17. "Patriarchal norms often create unequal emotional labor in relationships."
18. "The push for independence can sometimes conflict with the need for connection."

19. "Nonbinary and fluid gender roles offer freedom from outdated expectations."
20. "Society benefits when we redefine success for both genders beyond traditional markers."
21. "Women are no longer confined to supportive roles; they are equal contributors."
22. "Gender roles can serve as a starting point but should never limit individuality."
23. "The partnership model, rather than a power hierarchy, fosters healthier relationships."
24. "Men supporting gender equality benefit from richer, more meaningful relationships."
25. "Both genders thrive when given the freedom to embrace their unique qualities."

DATING IN THE DIGITAL AGE

Talking Points (201–225):

1. "Swipe culture has commodified love; how do we bring back depth?"
2. "Online dating creates opportunities but can also lead to superficial connections."
3. "The instant gratification of apps often conflicts with the patience real love requires."
4. "Catfishing and misrepresentation highlight the dangers of digital anonymity."
5. "Digital dating requires clear communication to build trust and authenticity."
6. "Social media often creates unrealistic expectations for modern relationships."
7. "Technology should facilitate connections, not replace meaningful interaction."
8. "Long-distance relationships are more feasible with technology but still require effort."

9. "Virtual connections lack the nuances of in-person chemistry and energy."
10. "The paradox of choice in dating apps often leads to indecision and dissatisfaction."
11. "Texting lacks tone and context, leading to miscommunication in budding relationships."
12. "Ghosting is a symptom of emotional immaturity in digital dating."
13. "Authenticity is often lost when people curate their dating profiles for approval."
14. "Navigating online dating successfully requires emotional intelligence and self-awareness."
15. "Love in the digital age needs to move beyond algorithms to genuine understanding."
16. "The fear of missing out often undermines commitment in the app-dating world."
17. "Dating apps should prioritize compatibility over appearance to foster meaningful matches."
18. "Technology offers convenience, but emotional connection remains timeless."
19. "Privacy and consent must be emphasized in digital dating spaces."
20. "Intentional dating helps combat the distractions of the digital age."
21. "Emotional availability is harder to gauge online than in person."
22. "Creating boundaries around technology fosters healthier dating dynamics."
23. "Video calls and voice notes can bridge the gap between virtual and real connection."
24. "Digital dating requires balancing openness with discernment."
25. "The ultimate goal is to transition from online interactions to real-world connection."

Subtopic: Unpacking Modern Relationship Dynamics

Host Script:

"Modern relationships come with unique challenges, from blurred boundaries to changing gender roles. How do we navigate these evolving dynamics while maintaining healthy, meaningful connections?"

Talking Points for Panelists:

1. "Boundaries in relationships are not walls; they are bridges that foster healthy connections by defining mutual respect."
2. "The rise of situationships reflects a societal fear of commitment and vulnerability, highlighting the need for clarity in intentions."
3. "Empathy is the cornerstone of any relationship, but it must be balanced with self-respect to prevent emotional burnout."
4. "Modern relationships thrive when both partners are emotionally intelligent and communicative."
5. "Power dynamics in relationships are shifting, requiring greater collaboration and mutual understanding."

Follow-Up Questions:

1. "What role do communication and boundaries play in creating and sustaining modern relationships?"
2. "How has the digital age reshaped traditional relationship dynamics, for better or worse?"
3. "What are the biggest challenges facing relationships today, and how can they be addressed?"
4. "How do societal expectations impact individuals' willingness to commit?"
5. "What steps can individuals take to transition from situationships to more defined, fulfilling relationships?"

SUBTOPIC: GENDER ROLES AND EXPECTATIONS

Host Script:

"Gender roles continue to evolve, challenging traditional expectations and reshaping how we relate to one another. How do we redefine these roles in ways that promote equity and authenticity?"

Talking Points for Panelists:

1. "Traditional gender roles often restrict emotional expression, especially for men, perpetuating unhealthy coping mechanisms."
2. "Feminism and masculinity are not adversaries; they are evolving paradigms seeking balance and mutual empowerment."
3. "Media plays a significant role in perpetuating or challenging outdated gender norms, influencing how individuals view themselves and others."

4. "Gender roles rooted in stereotypes limit potential—breaking free allows individuals to explore their true capabilities."
5. "The shift toward egalitarian relationships reflects society's growing emphasis on partnership over power hierarchies."

Follow-Up Questions:

1. "How can we encourage men to embrace vulnerability and emotional expression without fear of societal judgment?"
2. "What are some ways media can promote positive gender role models and challenge stereotypes?"
3. "How do cultural norms influence our perceptions of gender roles in relationships?"
4. "What role does education play in redefining gender expectations for future generations?"
5. "Can we truly achieve equality in relationships without addressing systemic issues tied to gender?"

10 QUICK PROMPT QUESTIONS

1. "What do healthy boundaries look like in modern relationships?"
2. "How do shifting gender roles impact your personal relationships?"
3. "What's a way couples can navigate the challenges of the digital age?"
4. "How can we balance empathy and self-respect in romantic partnerships?"
5. "Do you think the rise of situationships reflects a cultural fear of vulnerability?"
6. "What role does media play in shaping how we perceive gender and relationships?"
7. "How can men and women work together to redefine outdated gender expectations?"
8. "What's one way to promote vulnerability and emotional openness in men?"
9. "How has technology improved or hindered your ability to connect with others?"
10. "What's the most important lesson you've learned about balancing individual growth and partnership?"

CATERGORY FOUR: Identity and Society

BLACK IDENTITY AND REPRESENTATION

Talking Points (226–250):

1. "Representation in media is not diversity; it's the start of inclusion."
2. "Authentic Black representation must move beyond stereotypes and tokenism."
3. "Visibility matters—seeing oneself reflected in media shapes self-perception and aspirations."
4. "Diverse stories amplify the richness of Black experiences, challenging monolithic narratives."
5. "Representation should empower, not perpetuate harmful tropes or caricatures."
6. "Black creators must have the freedom to tell their own stories on their own terms."
7. "Representation in leadership positions drives systemic change and dismantles bias."
8. "The absence of Black voices in decision-making reinforces systemic inequities."
9. "Media platforms have a responsibility to uplift underrepresented voices."
10. "True representation includes acknowledging the diversity within the Black community."
11. "Representation in schools and education is vital for fostering self-esteem in Black youth."

12. "Corporate diversity initiatives often fail to address structural inequities."
13. "Inclusion is not just about being seen; it's about being valued and respected."
14. "Cultural appropriation diminishes the importance of authentic Black representation."
15. "Representation in politics directly impacts policies that affect Black communities."
16. "Black identity thrives when there is space for both individuality and collective solidarity."
17. "The fight for representation must extend to marginalized subgroups within Black communities."
18. "Black joy and success deserve as much media attention as Black pain and struggle."
19. "Representation should highlight both history and the ongoing contributions of Black people."
20. "Black excellence should not be an anomaly but a normalized expectation."
21. "The erasure of Black voices in history perpetuates systemic oppression."
22. "Nuanced storytelling challenges the systemic bias embedded in mainstream media."
23. "Representation without empowerment risks becoming performative."
24. "Celebrating Black culture requires understanding and respecting its origins."
25. "Representation is a tool for liberation, but it must be accompanied by systemic change."

CULTURAL PRESSURES AND RESPECTABILITY POLITICS

Talking Points (251–275):

1. "Respectability politics are a survival tool, but do they serve growth?"
2. "The pressure to conform to societal norms often erases individuality within Black identity."
3. "Respectability politics historically sought to counter stereotypes but often reinforced others."
4. "Success within systemic frameworks doesn't equate to liberation."
5. "Authenticity should never be sacrificed for the sake of acceptability."
6. "Respectability politics often ask marginalized groups to bear the burden of systemic change."
7. "Adhering to respectability can perpetuate internalized oppression."
8. "The concept of 'fitting in' often undermines the fight for true equality."
9. "Respectability does not protect Black people from systemic racism or discrimination."
10. "The expectation of perfection is a heavy burden placed on Black professionals."
11. "Dress codes and language policing are tools of respectability politics that limit individuality."
12. "The policing of Black expression, from hairstyles to vernacular, reflects systemic bias."
13. "Challenging respectability politics requires reclaiming and redefining cultural norms."
14. "Respectability politics often silence the voices of those most in need of representation."
15. "True equity values authenticity over conformity."

16. "Generational divides often arise around the expectations of respectability."
17. "Respectability politics ignore the systemic nature of oppression, placing undue blame on individuals."
18. "Empowerment comes from rejecting respectability and embracing individuality."
19. "Respectability often creates divisions within the Black community rather than uniting it."
20. "Radical self-expression is a powerful form of resistance."
21. "Liberation requires dismantling the frameworks that uphold respectability politics."
22. "The double standard of respectability for Black men and women exacerbates inequality."
23. "Embracing cultural heritage without fear is the antithesis of respectability politics."
24. "Respectability politics are a response to oppression but often uphold it."
25. "Empowering future generations means rejecting conformity as a measure of success."

THE INTERSECTION OF COLORISM AND PRIVILEGE

Talking Points (276–300):

1. "Colorism isn't just about skin tone; it's about power dynamics."
2. "Lighter skin privilege reinforces the hierarchies created by systemic racism."
3. "The roots of colorism stem from colonialism and the privileging of whiteness."
4. "Colorism affects access to opportunities, beauty standards, and social mobility."
5. "Challenging colorism requires recognizing it within and beyond the Black community."

6. "Representation should reflect the full spectrum of Black beauty and identity."
7. "Colorism divides communities, creating barriers to solidarity and collective action."
8. "Media perpetuates colorism by prioritizing lighter-skinned individuals in roles and representation."
9. "Dark-skinned individuals often face harsher treatment in societal, professional, and legal contexts."
10. "Colorism is a form of systemic oppression that thrives on proximity to whiteness."
11. "The erasure of darker-skinned people from history perpetuates colorist narratives."
12. "Celebrating darker-skinned individuals challenges entrenched beauty standards."
13. "Colorism impacts mental health, fostering feelings of inadequacy and exclusion."
14. "Addressing colorism requires open, honest conversations within communities."
15. "Privilege within communities should be acknowledged and leveraged to dismantle colorism."
16. "Dark-skinned women often face a double bias due to both gender and skin tone."
17. "Colorism reinforces socioeconomic disparities, creating cycles of inequality."
18. "Educating younger generations is key to breaking the cycle of colorism."
19. "Challenging Eurocentric beauty standards is essential in addressing colorism."
20. "Colorism affects not only Black communities but other communities of color globally."
21. "Intersectionality highlights how colorism compounds with other forms of discrimination."
22. "Accountability is crucial for dismantling colorism, especially within media and institutions."

23. "Healing from colorism begins with self-acceptance and cultural pride."
24. "Confronting internalized colorism is just as important as addressing external bias."
25. "True equity embraces the beauty, talent, and contributions of all skin tones."

Subtopic: Black Identity and Representation

Host Script:

"Representation matters, but is it enough? Seeing Black faces in media and leadership is a start, but true progress lies in achieving equity. Let's dive into what true equity looks like for Black identity in media and society and how we can move beyond performative gestures to meaningful change."

Talking Points for Panelists:

1. "Diversity without equity is performative; it must lead to systemic change, addressing structural barriers that hinder progress."
2. "Black identity is not monolithic, yet media often portrays it as such, failing to capture the richness and diversity of experiences within the community."
3. "Cultural appropriation vs. appreciation—where do we draw the line? True appreciation honors the origins and contributions of Black culture without exploitation."
4. "Representation in leadership positions ensures that Black voices are shaping narratives, not just appearing in them."
5. "Authentic Black representation challenges stereotypes and celebrates multidimensional characters and stories."

Follow-Up Questions:

1. "How does the lack of representation in media, leadership, and education impact self-identity for Black individuals, especially youth?"
2. "What steps can industries take to ensure authentic representation that uplifts and empowers Black voices?"
3. "How can communities hold media accountable for perpetuating harmful stereotypes?"
4. "What role do allies play in supporting authentic representation and equity for Black identity?"
5. "How do we balance celebrating Black culture with protecting it from exploitation or misrepresentation?"

10 QUICK PROMPT QUESTIONS

1. "What does authentic Black representation look like to you?"
2. "How can diversity efforts move beyond surface-level inclusion?"
3. "What impact does media portrayal have on shaping Black identity?"
4. "How do stereotypes in media perpetuate systemic inequities?"
5. "What's the difference between cultural appropriation and appreciation, and how can we define the line?"
6. "How can storytelling in media better reflect the diversity within the Black community?"
7. "Why is it important to have Black leadership in industries that shape cultural narratives?"
8. "How does representation—or the lack of it—affect the mental health of Black individuals?"
9. "What role do allies and advocates play in ensuring equitable representation?"
10. "What steps can schools and education systems take to better represent Black history and culture?"

CATERGORY FIVE: Social and Economic Structures

THE WEALTH GAP AND GENERATIONAL CYCLES

Talking Points (301–325):

1. "Generational wealth starts with generational education—knowledge is the first currency."
2. "Systemic barriers prevent many families from breaking the cycle of poverty."
3. "Wealth inequality is often reinforced through policies that favor the already privileged."
4. "Financial literacy is key to breaking generational cycles of economic struggle."
5. "Homeownership is a cornerstone of generational wealth but remains out of reach for many."
6. "The racial wealth gap persists due to unequal access to resources and opportunities."
7. "Building wealth requires long-term planning, yet many face the immediate pressure of survival."
8. "Generational cycles of poverty are perpetuated by lack of access to equitable education."
9. "Economic policies often favor corporations over individuals, widening the wealth gap."
10. "Inheriting debt is as much a generational cycle as inheriting wealth."

11. "Economic stability for one generation can create opportunities for the next."
12. "The wealth gap isn't just about money; it's about access to healthcare, education, and security."
13. "Systemic racism plays a significant role in the racial wealth gap."
14. "Generational cycles can be broken by investing in underserved communities."
15. "The wealth gap is an indicator of systemic inequality, not individual failure."
16. "Access to affordable childcare is a critical factor in building economic stability."
17. "Wealth inequality limits social mobility and stifles innovation."
18. "Economic empowerment begins with equitable wages and opportunities."
19. "Wealth redistribution policies can help close the generational wealth gap."
20. "The role of community support systems in building wealth is often underestimated."
21. "Entrepreneurship offers a path to generational wealth but requires access to capital."
22. "Redlining and housing discrimination have long-term effects on wealth accumulation."
23. "Economic stability is a foundation for mental and physical health."
24. "Breaking cycles of poverty requires a collective effort from communities and policymakers."
25. "Generational wealth is more than money; it's about creating a legacy of opportunity."

EDUCATION AND ITS SOCIETAL IMPACTS

Talking Points (326–350):

1. "Standardized testing is a measure of privilege, not potential."
2. "Education is the great equalizer only when access is truly equitable."
3. "Public schools in underserved areas often lack the resources needed for student success."
4. "Investing in early childhood education yields long-term societal benefits."
5. "Education systems often reinforce systemic inequalities instead of dismantling them."
6. "School funding tied to property taxes perpetuates cycles of inequality."
7. "Access to higher education remains a barrier for many due to cost and systemic bias."
8. "Curriculums must reflect diverse histories and perspectives to be truly inclusive."
9. "The school-to-prison pipeline highlights the failure of educational systems to serve marginalized communities."
10. "Education should focus on critical thinking and creativity, not rote memorization."
11. "Teachers are underpaid and undervalued despite their critical role in shaping society."
12. "College degrees are no longer a guaranteed pathway to economic success."
13. "Education reform must address both curriculum and systemic inequities."
14. "Digital divides exacerbate educational disparities in an increasingly tech-driven world."

15. "Access to mentorship programs can change the trajectory of a student's life."
16. "Overemphasis on test scores ignores other valuable forms of intelligence."
17. "The rising cost of education perpetuates student debt cycles."
18. "Lack of representation among educators impacts student engagement and achievement."
19. "Vocational training and trade schools should be valued as much as traditional education."
20. "Social-emotional learning is as important as academics in shaping well-rounded individuals."
21. "Inclusive education policies benefit society by fostering empathy and understanding."
22. "Education systems must prepare students for a rapidly changing global economy."
23. "Parental involvement in education is critical but often limited by economic barriers."
24. "Equitable education systems create opportunities for generational change."
25. "Access to quality education is a human right, not a privilege."

GENTRIFICATION AND ITS DOUBLE EDGES

Talking Points (351–375):

1. "Gentrification can build communities or displace them—what's the balance?"
2. "Economic development should prioritize the needs of existing residents."
3. "Affordable housing must be central to any gentrification effort to prevent displacement."
4. "Gentrification often erases cultural heritage, replacing it with homogeneity."

5. "The influx of wealth in gentrified areas rarely benefits longtime residents."
6. "Community-driven development models offer a solution to harmful gentrification."
7. "Displacement due to gentrification perpetuates cycles of poverty."
8. "Urban renewal projects often prioritize profits over people."
9. "Access to public spaces must remain equitable as neighborhoods change."
10. "Gentrification can widen the wealth gap by driving up property values and rents."
11. "The voices of residents must be included in urban planning decisions."
12. "Gentrification often leads to cultural appropriation of historically marginalized communities."
13. "Investments in infrastructure should benefit everyone, not just newcomers."
14. "Gentrification disproportionately affects communities of color."
15. "Economic incentives for developers should include requirements for affordable housing."
16. "Small businesses often face extinction when gentrification drives up costs."
17. "The loss of community networks due to gentrification has long-term social impacts."
18. "Gentrification can create opportunities but must be managed with equity in mind."
19. "Community land trusts are a powerful tool to prevent displacement."
20. "Residents must be educated about their rights in gentrifying neighborhoods."
21. "The cultural vibrancy of a neighborhood often attracts gentrification, only for it to be lost."

22. "Gentrification highlights the need for broader systemic housing reform."
23. "Equity in urban planning requires proactive policies, not reactive measures."
24. "Revitalization without displacement is possible but requires intentionality."
25. "Balancing economic growth with social justice is the key to ethical urban development."

Subtopic: The Wealth Gap and Generational Cycle

Host Script:

"The wealth gap continues to widen, leaving marginalized communities trapped in cycles of poverty. How do we address systemic barriers to economic mobility, and what steps can be taken to build generational wealth?"

Talking Points for Panelists:

1. "Generational wealth begins with access to education, financial literacy, and equitable opportunities."
2. "The racial wealth gap is a product of systemic policies, including redlining and discriminatory lending practices."
3. "Homeownership remains a cornerstone of wealth building, but systemic inequities make it inaccessible for many."
4. "Breaking generational cycles of poverty requires community investment and policy reform."
5. "Financial literacy should be taught early, as it is a foundational tool for long-term economic stability."
6. "Generational debt is a major obstacle to economic progress in underserved communities."
7. "Small business ownership can be a pathway to wealth but requires access to capital and resources."

8. "The wealth gap is not just an individual problem but a structural one that demands systemic solutions."
9. "Building generational wealth requires dismantling barriers to equitable wages and job opportunities."
10. "Wealth redistribution policies, such as reparations, are essential for addressing historical inequities."

Follow-Up Questions:

1. "What role does financial literacy play in addressing the wealth gap, and how can it be more widely taught?"
2. "How do systemic barriers like redlining continue to affect generational wealth in marginalized communities?"
3. "What policies could effectively close the racial wealth gap in the next decade?"
4. "How can small businesses in underserved communities be better supported to build wealth locally?"
5. "What are the biggest obstacles to homeownership, and how can they be addressed equitably?"

SUBTOPIC 2: EDUCATION AND ITS SOCIETAL IMPACTS

Host Script:

"Education is often seen as the great equalizer, but systemic inequities in access and quality suggest otherwise. How can we reform education systems to serve as a true catalyst for social and economic mobility?"

Talking Points for Panelists:

1. "Standardized testing often measures privilege more than potential, reinforcing inequities."
2. "Access to early childhood education has a profound impact on long-term societal outcomes."
3. "Funding education through property taxes perpetuates cycles of inequality in low-income communities."
4. "Curriculums must include diverse perspectives to reflect the histories and contributions of all groups."
5. "Digital access is no longer a luxury but a necessity for equitable education."
6. "Vocational training and trade schools should be equally valued as traditional higher education pathways."
7. "The school-to-prison pipeline highlights the intersection of education and systemic inequities."
8. "Teacher pay and support must reflect the critical role they play in shaping society."
9. "Education reform must address systemic racism embedded in school policies and practices."
10. "Mentorship programs can bridge the gap for students in underserved communities, providing guidance and opportunity."

Follow-Up Questions:

1. "How do property tax-based school funding models perpetuate educational inequality?"
2. "What are the benefits of diversifying curriculums, and how can schools implement this change?"
3. "How can technology be leveraged to close the digital divide in underserved schools?"

4. "What role do teachers play in addressing systemic inequities, and how can we better support them?"
5. "How can mentorship programs or community involvement improve outcomes for students in low-income areas?"

SUBTOPIC 3: GENTRIFICATION AND ITS DOUBLE EDGES

Host Script:

"Gentrification is often framed as revitalization, but it comes with consequences, particularly for marginalized communities. How can we balance economic development with equity and inclusion?"

Talking Points for Panelists:

1. "Gentrification can uplift neighborhoods economically but often displaces longtime residents."
2. "Affordable housing policies must accompany development projects to ensure inclusivity."
3. "Revitalization efforts should be led by community voices, not just external investors."
4. "Preserving the cultural identity of neighborhoods is essential in any development effort."
5. "Community land trusts are an effective tool for preventing displacement and promoting equity."
6. "Small businesses are often casualties of gentrification, requiring targeted support to survive."
7. "Public infrastructure improvements should prioritize accessibility for existing residents."
8. "Economic growth should not come at the cost of community cohesion and cultural heritage."

9. "Gentrification highlights the need for systemic reform in housing policies and urban planning."
10. "True revitalization balances economic growth with the needs and rights of all residents."

Follow-Up Questions:

1. "How can cities prioritize affordable housing while pursuing economic development?"
2. "What role should community members play in shaping revitalization projects in their neighborhoods?"
3. "How can small businesses be supported to survive and thrive in gentrifying areas?"
4. "What strategies can urban planners use to preserve cultural heritage in changing neighborhoods?"
5. "How do we prevent displacement while encouraging economic investment in underserved communities?"

10 QUICK PROMPT QUESTIONS

1. "What steps can individuals take to build generational wealth in the face of systemic barriers?"
2. "How does the wealth gap affect social mobility and opportunity in marginalized communities?"
3. "What reforms are most urgently needed to make education a true equalizer?"
4. "How can technology address educational inequities in underserved areas?"
5. "What role does cultural preservation play in discussions about gentrification?"
6. "How can cities ensure economic development benefits existing residents, not just newcomers?"
7. "What is one practical way to address the racial wealth gap in your community?"
8. "How does the school-to-prison pipeline highlight failures of the education system?"
9. "What policies could make homeownership more accessible to historically excluded groups?"
10. "What's the balance between revitalizing neighborhoods and preserving their cultural identity?"

CATERGORY SIX: Feminism and Masculinity

MODERN FEMINISM VS. TRADITIONAL ROLES

Talking Points (376–400):

1. "Feminism isn't about rejecting men but rejecting oppression and inequality."
2. "Modern feminism seeks to create partnerships between genders, not hierarchies."
3. "Traditional gender roles can provide structure but often limit individual freedom."
4. "The feminist movement evolves as societal needs and expectations change."
5. "Feminism is as much about dismantling patriarchy as it is about empowering all genders."
6. "Equality doesn't mean sameness; it means valuing diverse contributions equally."
7. "Traditional roles often reinforce dependency; feminism advocates for independence and collaboration."
8. "Feminism isn't just a women's issue; it benefits everyone by promoting equity."
9. "Intersectional feminism addresses the unique challenges faced by women of color, LGBTQ+ individuals, and other marginalized groups."
10. "Empowering women doesn't diminish men; it creates stronger communities."

11. "Feminism challenges the unpaid labor expectations often placed on women in traditional roles."
12. "Society thrives when everyone is free to pursue their full potential, unrestricted by outdated norms."
13. "Modern feminism recognizes the value of choice—whether in careers, parenting, or lifestyle."
14. "The fight for gender equality must also address issues like pay gaps, workplace discrimination, and domestic violence."
15. "Traditional roles can coexist with feminism when chosen freely, not imposed by societal expectations."
16. "Feminism pushes for systemic change, not just individual empowerment."
17. "Advocating for gender equity includes addressing global disparities in education, healthcare, and opportunities."
18. "Men and women both face unique pressures from traditional roles, making feminism relevant to all."
19. "Redefining masculinity and femininity as fluid concepts fosters greater understanding and equality."
20. "Feminism seeks to balance the scales, not tip them in favor of one group over another."
21. "The role of allies in the feminist movement is critical for creating broader cultural shifts."
22. "Traditional roles can stifle creativity and innovation by restricting who can participate in various fields."
23. "Feminism isn't a rejection of family values; it's a call to redefine them in inclusive ways."
24. "Empathy and collaboration are hallmarks of modern feminism, moving away from divisive narratives."
25. "The ultimate goal of feminism is a society where gender is not a barrier to opportunity."

TOXIC MASCULINITY AND ITS HEALING

Talking Points (401–425):

1. "Toxic masculinity isn't about men being bad; it's about harmful conditioning that limits emotional expression."
2. "Healing toxic masculinity starts with creating safe spaces for vulnerability."
3. "Toxic masculinity pressures men to suppress their emotions, leading to mental health challenges."
4. "Society often punishes men for stepping outside traditional norms, reinforcing toxic behaviors."
5. "Healthy masculinity embraces both strength and sensitivity as complementary traits."
6. "Toxic masculinity harms men as much as it harms the people around them."
7. "Breaking the cycle of toxic masculinity requires teaching boys emotional intelligence early on."
8. "Patriarchal systems enforce toxic masculinity by equating dominance with success."
9. "Healing masculinity involves redefining strength as resilience, compassion, and accountability."
10. "Media representations of men as solely stoic or aggressive perpetuate harmful stereotypes."
11. "Fathers and male role models play a key role in challenging toxic norms."
12. "Addressing toxic masculinity is not an attack on men but a call to liberate them from restrictive expectations."
13. "Men who embrace emotional vulnerability often experience deeper, more meaningful relationships."
14. "Toxic masculinity can create a culture of violence by associating aggression with masculinity."

15. "Society must value men for who they are, not just what they achieve."
16. "Men's mental health is often overlooked because of societal expectations to 'be tough.'"
17. "Healing masculinity involves fostering empathy and collaboration, not competition."
18. "The concept of 'boys will be boys' perpetuates harmful behaviors instead of addressing accountability."
19. "Men must be included as allies and participants in conversations about gender equality."
20. "Deconstructing toxic masculinity is about offering men freedom to define themselves authentically."
21. "Education systems can play a role in teaching healthy expressions of masculinity from a young age."
22. "Communities thrive when men are empowered to support and uplift others, not dominate them."
23. "Therapy and support groups can be transformative for men healing from toxic societal pressures."
24. "Healthy masculinity contributes to stronger partnerships, families, and communities."
25. "The journey to healing masculinity is about replacing fear and dominance with love and understanding."

Subtopic: Toxic Masculinity and Its Healing

HOST SCRIPT:
"Toxic masculinity has long been a barrier to emotional expression and healthy relationships. It stems from societal pressures and expectations that define manhood in restrictive ways. How can we move from toxic masculinity to a healthier, more inclusive definition of manhood that benefits everyone?"

Talking Points for Panelists:

1. "Toxic masculinity stems from fear—of vulnerability, emotion, and change. It teaches men to equate strength with suppression and dominance."
2. "Healing masculinity requires creating safe spaces for emotional expression where men feel supported, not judged, for sharing their feelings."
3. "Fathers and male mentors play a critical role in reshaping masculine norms by modeling healthy behaviors and showing that vulnerability is a strength, not a weakness."
4. "Redefining masculinity means embracing qualities like empathy, collaboration, and emotional resilience alongside traditional traits like confidence and leadership."
5. "The media's role in perpetuating or challenging toxic masculinity cannot be underestimated; representation matters."

Follow-Up Questions:

1. "What does healthy masculinity look like in today's
   social climate, and how does it differ from traditional
   ideals of manhood?"
2. "How can communities—both men and women—support men in unlearning harmful behaviors and adopt-
   ing healthier practices?"
3. "What role do schools and educators play in teaching
   boys to embrace emotional intelligence and vulnerability?"
4. "How can we encourage men to seek mental health
   support without the stigma often associated with it?"
5. "What practical steps can fathers and male mentors
   take to model healthier versions of masculinity for
   younger generations?"

10 QUICK PROMPTS

1. "What's one way we can redefine masculinity to include emotional vulnerability?"
2. "How does toxic masculinity negatively impact men's mental health?"
3. "What role do fathers and male mentors play in shaping healthier ideas of masculinity?"
4. "How can society better support men in expressing emotions without fear of judgment?"
5. "What does a healthy, inclusive definition of manhood look like to you?"
6. "How can media and entertainment challenge toxic masculinity and promote positive role models?"
7. "What are the biggest barriers men face when trying to unlearn toxic behaviors?"
8. "How can schools and educators encourage boys to embrace emotional intelligence?"
9. "What steps can communities take to create safe spaces for men to explore healthy masculinity?"
10. "How does the concept of 'man up' harm men and limit their growth?"

CATERGORY SEVEN: Youth and Elders

The Generational Divide

Talking Points (426–450):

1. "Wisdom isn't outdated; it's just waiting for the right ears."
2. "Generational differences are opportunities for growth, not conflict."
3. "Each generation's challenges shape its values and perspectives."
4. "Bridging the generational divide requires empathy and active listening."
5. "Technology has widened the gap but can also serve as a bridge."
6. "Younger generations bring innovation, while older generations bring experience—both are essential."
7. "Respecting differences in communication styles can foster better understanding."
8. "Generational stereotypes limit meaningful dialogue and perpetuate conflict."
9. "Mentorship programs create valuable connections between youth and elders."
10. "Both generations benefit from sharing their stories and learning from each other."
11. "The divide often stems from misunderstandings, not irreconcilable differences."

12. "Acknowledging mutual frustrations opens the door to constructive dialogue."
13. "Historical context helps younger generations understand the struggles of their elders."
14. "The energy of youth and the patience of age can create powerful partnerships."
15. "Generational divides weaken when both sides seek to understand rather than judge."
16. "Intergenerational collaboration is crucial for addressing societal challenges."
17. "Elders can learn adaptability from youth, while youth can learn resilience from elders."
18. "Bridging the gap is about shared goals, not agreeing on everything."
19. "The divide often reflects changes in cultural, technological, and societal norms."
20. "Mutual respect is the foundation of any effort to close the generational gap."
21. "Youth and elders are allies, not adversaries, in creating a better future."
22. "Generations should celebrate their differences as strengths, not barriers."
23. "Intergenerational understanding enriches both personal and professional relationships."
24. "Younger voices bring fresh ideas, while older voices provide context and wisdom."
25. "The best solutions often emerge when generations work together."

Social Media's Influence on the Younger Generation

Talking Points (451–475):

1. "The algorithm isn't neutral; it reflects and shapes culture."
2. "Social media amplifies voices but also distorts reality."
3. "Younger generations are the most connected yet often feel the most isolated."
4. "The comparison culture fueled by social media undermines self-esteem."
5. "Social media literacy is essential for navigating misinformation and harmful content."
6. "The internet has democratized information but blurred the line between fact and opinion."
7. "Viral trends can spark positive movements or create toxic pressures."
8. "Social media has empowered youth activism like never before."
9. "Screen time must be balanced with offline experiences to foster mental well-being."
10. "Algorithms are designed to capture attention, often prioritizing engagement over truth."
11. "Social media can be a tool for connection or a source of anxiety, depending on how it's used."
12. "Online platforms provide creative outlets for youth but also expose them to cyberbullying."
13. "The rapid pace of online trends can lead to burnout and overstimulation."
14. "Authenticity on social media is often replaced by carefully curated personas."
15. "Youth need guidance on building healthy boundaries with technology."
16. "Influencers shape the values and aspirations of younger generations, for better or worse."

17. "The digital age has redefined what it means to grow up."
18. "Social media fosters global awareness but can also create echo chambers."
19. "Critical thinking skills are more important than ever in the age of social media."
20. "Social media is a tool, not a replacement for genuine human connection."
21. "Parents and educators must engage in conversations about online behavior and consequences."
22. "Youth-led social movements thrive on social media, highlighting its potential for good."
23. "Privacy concerns are growing as social media collects and monetizes personal data."
24. "The addictive nature of platforms makes it harder for youth to disconnect."
25. "Empowering youth to control their digital presence builds confidence and autonomy."

The Role of Elders in Modern Society

Talking Points (476–500):

1. "Elders are the keepers of tradition; how do we invite them back to the table?"
2. "Their wisdom provides context for understanding today's challenges."
3. "The marginalization of elders robs society of valuable experience and insight."
4. "Intergenerational relationships foster mutual respect and learning."
5. "Elders play a critical role in preserving cultural heritage."
6. "They offer perspective and patience that only come with time."

7. "Modern society often undervalues elders, focusing instead on youth-centric ideals."
8. "Elders provide stability in times of uncertainty, drawing from their lived experiences."
9. "Programs that integrate elders into schools, workplaces, and communities benefit all generations."
10. "Their life lessons can inspire resilience and adaptability in younger generations."
11. "Elders serve as mentors, offering guidance that transcends textbooks."
12. "They bridge the past and present, connecting historical knowledge with modern innovation."
13. "Elder voices in leadership roles bring balance to decision-making processes."
14. "The wisdom of elders can guide youth in avoiding the mistakes of the past."
15. "Societies that revere their elders tend to maintain stronger cultural identities."
16. "Elders teach patience and the value of long-term thinking in an era of instant gratification."
17. "They remind us that progress is rooted in understanding history."
18. "Elders offer unique insights into the consequences of societal trends."
19. "Creating platforms for elders to share their stories enriches community bonds."
20. "The role of elders in storytelling preserves history and inspires future generations."
21. "They provide moral and ethical guidance grounded in experience."
22. "Elders in leadership roles model humility and service for younger generations."
23. "Programs that connect elders with youth reduce generational loneliness and isolation."

24. "Their wisdom can shape policy decisions that account for long-term impact."
25. "A society that values its elders ensures a stronger foundation for future generations."

Subtopic: The Influence of Algorithms on Culture

Host Script:

"Algorithms are a driving force behind much of what we see, hear, and even believe. They don't just reflect culture—they shape it. What responsibility do tech companies have in managing this influence, and how can we as individuals navigate this algorithm-driven world responsibly?"

Talking Points for Panelists:

1. "Algorithms amplify what they're fed—bias, misinformation, or positivity—making it crucial to scrutinize the inputs."
2. "Social media platforms must prioritize transparency about how algorithms work to build trust and accountability."
3. "We, as users, also have the power to curate our feeds by engaging with content that aligns with our values, subtly influencing the algorithm."
4. "Algorithms can create echo chambers, but with awareness, users can seek out diverse perspectives."
5. "Tech companies must acknowledge their role in shaping public opinion and take active steps to prevent harm."

6. "The monetization of engagement often prioritizes sensational content over accurate or constructive information."
7. "Educating users on how algorithms function empowers them to make informed decisions."
8. "Algorithms should promote meaningful connections rather than exploit divisiveness for profit."
9. "Balancing freedom of expression with the responsibility to reduce harm is a major challenge for tech platforms."
10. "Public pressure and regulatory measures are essential for holding tech companies accountable."

Follow-Up Questions:

1. "How can individuals critically evaluate the content they consume in an algorithm-driven media landscape?"
2. "What regulations or ethical standards should be in place to prevent harmful effects of algorithms on society?"
3. "How do algorithms contribute to echo chambers, and what can users do to break out of them?"
4. "What role should tech companies play in curating content responsibly while respecting free speech?"
5. "How can we promote media literacy to help users navigate the complexities of algorithm-driven platforms?"

10 QUICK PROMPT QUESTIONS

- "How do algorithms shape the way we perceive the world?"
- "What steps can individuals take to avoid falling into algorithm-driven echo chambers?"
- "How can social media platforms ensure their algorithms promote positivity instead of misinformation?"
- "What are some examples of how algorithms have influenced culture for better or worse?"
- "What responsibility do tech companies have in managing the ethical implications of their algorithms?"
- "How can users curate their feeds to create a more balanced digital experience?"
- "What impact do algorithms have on creativity and innovation in content creation?"
- "Should algorithms be regulated, and if so, what would effective regulation look like?"
- "How can greater transparency from tech companies improve trust in their platforms?"
- "What role does media literacy play in helping people navigate algorithm-driven content?"

CONCLUSION

As we've explored the multifaceted topics in this guide, it's clear that addressing social climate issues requires more than conversation—it demands action, empathy, and continued learning. These talking points are designed to serve as catalysts for meaningful dialogue, but the true power lies in translating those dialogues into change.

Reflecting on Inspiration and Change

- Conversations rooted in understanding can break down barriers, challenge biases, and spark innovative solutions.
- Each talking point highlights a critical aspect of our society, from personal empowerment and relationships to systemic inequalities and cultural shifts.
- By reflecting on these issues, we can to identify actionable steps, whether that's advocating for policy reform, fostering intergenerational collaboration, or amplifying underrepresented voices.

Encouraging Action and Growth

- **Engage:** Use these insights to foster discussions in your communities, workplaces, and personal networks. Start small—change often begins with one conversation.
- **Learn:** Commit to lifelong learning. Dive deeper into the topics that resonate most with you. Explore books, podcasts, and workshops to expand your understanding.

- **Act:** Channel insights into tangible actions. Support organizations, mentor others, participate in advocacy efforts, and practice accountability in your sphere of influence.
- **Collaborate:** True change is collective. Seek partnerships across generations, cultures, and ideologies to create inclusive and sustainable solutions.